MW01602103

SOUND*f*ORTH

SINGING I GO

vocal duets

ISBN 0-89084-882-3

Cover design by Andy Heckathorne

What If It Were Today?

Lelia N. Morris

Lelia N. Morris
Arranged by Fred and Ruth Coleman

Singing I Go

Eliza E. Hewitt

William J. Kirkpatrick
Arranged by Marta C. Murray

Gently flowing ♩. = 66

Voice I *mf*

The trust - ing heart to Je - sus clings, Nor an - y ill for - bodes, But at the cross of Cal - v'ry sings, Praise God for lift - ed

Piano *mf*

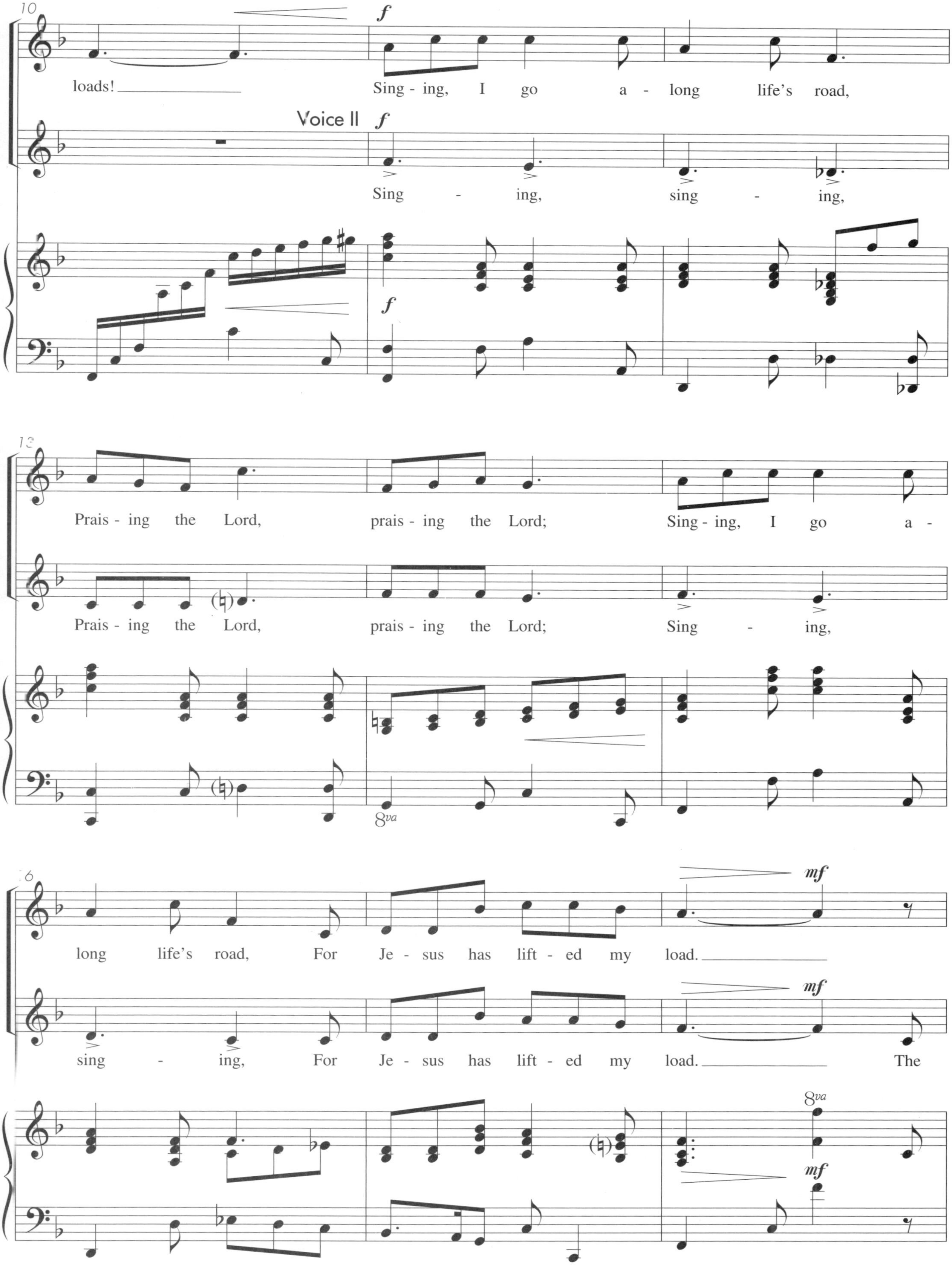
10
loads!
Sing - ing, I go a - long life's road,
Voice II
f
Sing - ing, sing - ing,
f
13
Prais - ing the Lord, prais - ing the Lord; Sing - ing, I go a -
Prais - ing the Lord, prais - ing the Lord; Sing - ing,
8va
16
long life's road, For Je - sus has lift - ed my load.
mf
sing - ing, For Je - sus has lift - ed my load. The
mf
8va
mf

Jesus Loves Even Me

Philip P. Bliss

Philip P. Bliss
Arranged by Joyce Oshiro

Surrender Medley

Elisha A. Hoffman

Elisha A. Hoffman
Arranged by Peter Davis

laid? Your heart, does the Spir - it con - trol?_____ You can

laid? Your heart, does the Spir - it con - trol?_____ You can

on - ly be blest and have peace and sweet rest, As you

on - ly be blest and have peace and sweet rest, As you

yield Him your bod - y and soul._____

yield Him your bod - y and soul._____

Slightly less motion

Slightly less motion

bless - ed Sav - ior, I sur - ren - der all.

bless - ed Sav - ior, I sur - ren - der all.

Since I fixed my eyes on Je - sus, I've lost sight of all be - side;

So en - chained my spir - it's vi - sion, Look - ing at the Cru - ci - fied.

Only a Sinner

James M. Gray

Karen Kuehmann

now I'm a sin-ner saved by His grace! _____

now I'm a sin-ner saved by His grace! _____

Suf-fer a sin-ner whose heart o-ver-flows, Lov-ing his Sav-ior to

Suf-fer a sin-ner whose heart o-ver-flows, Lov-ing his Sav-ior to

tell what he knows; Once more to tell it would I em-brace— I'm

tell what he knows; Once more to tell it would I em-brace— I'm

on-ly a sin-ner saved by His grace!_____ On-ly a sin-ner

on-ly a sin-ner saved by His grace!_____ On-ly a sin-ner

saved by His grace! On-ly a sin-ner saved by His grace!

saved by His grace! On-ly a sin-ner saved by His grace!

This is my sto-ry, to God be the glo-ry— I'm

This is my sto-ry, to God be the glo-ry— I'm

Give of Your Best to the Master

Howard B. Grose

Joan J. Pinkston

Joy to the World

Isaac Watts

Karen Kuehmann

Proclaim the Lofty Praise

Sarah Judson

Judith W. Rea

Triumphant, bright ♩ = 112

Voice I: Pro - claim the loft - y praise of Him who once___ was slain, But now is ris'n, through end - less days, In

Voice II: Pro - claim the loft - y praise of Him who once___ was slain, But now is ris'n, through end - less days, In

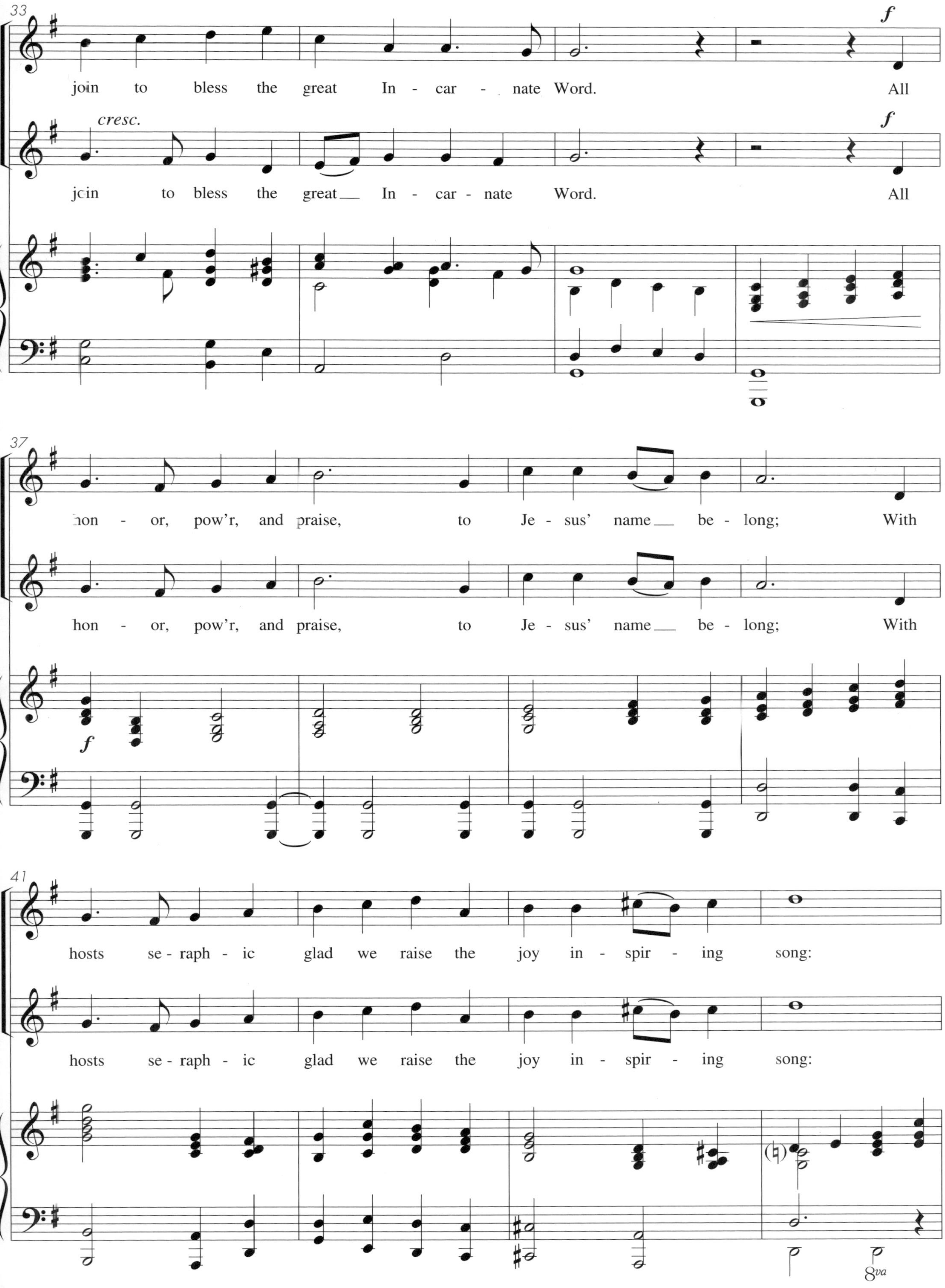

join to bless the great In - car - nate Word.   All

cresc.

join to bless the great In - car - nate Word.   All

hon - or, pow'r, and praise,   to Je - sus' name be - long;   With

hon - or, pow'r, and praise,   to Je - sus' name be - long;   With

hosts se - raph - ic glad we raise the joy in - spir - ing song:

hosts se - raph - ic glad we raise the joy in - spir - ing song:

8va

INDEX